Survive the Modern World

How
to start
A SIDE
Hustle

Kaylene Langford

Hardie Grant

BOOKS

Chapter One

NOW IS The Perfect Time To Start Your SIDE HUSTLE

A YEAR
from now
you'll wish you
STARTED
today ✳

Karen Lamb

There has never been a more convenient time to start a side hustle. People everywhere are taking their passions, natural abilities and skillsets and turning them into viable businesses and successful companies. A side hustle, according to the Cambridge Advanced Learner's Dictionary, is 'a piece of work or a job that you get paid for doing in addition to doing your main job'. Some people are content to always keep their side hustle as something that makes them a bit of extra money, while others aim to build their side hustle into their main hustle, going on to build thriving companies and long careers. Whichever way you lean, this book will help guide you through.

Not that long ago, working for ourselves was the norm for most people. Humans dwelled in small communities in which members used their natural skillsets to contribute to the maintenance and perpetuation of the village. People worked according to the hours of daylight and to the seasons. They were connected to the land and they mostly valued their time off, family connections and the wellbeing of their community.

Around 1750, the Industrial Revolution brought on the invention of machines, leading to the automation of production for almost all goods, including clothes, food and everyday tools. With the invention of steam trains, telephones and the banking system, business owners were given access to a global marketplace, enabling them to source, produce and sell goods and services at a considerably faster rate, increasing profits.

People left their villages, farms and communities to find work in factories, where they performed repetitive tasks for which they were paid very little. As a result, small-scale manufacturing and artisan crafts were replaced by large-scale industrial manufacturing.

A 2018 study conducted by Harvard Business Review concluded that being forced to leave autonomous, self-created lives to work mundane jobs under constant supervision for minimal wages led to a clear decline in the physical and mental wellbeing of the population.

Societies in the 21st century are still being shaped by that significant period in human history.

Today, a new reality is emerging. One where people are moving away from industrial mindsets, and changing their views on the necessity of working for someone else, doing uninteresting, repetitive tasks that affect one's emotional and physical wellbeing.

We are living in a time when we can easily connect to the entire globe. We have an ever-growing bank of innovative technologies, resources, apps and experts at our fingertips.

Never before have we been able to so easily communicate across the world without leaving the comfort of our homes, and at no cost. Platforms like Instagram, Facebook, WhatsApp, Twitter, Pinterest, TikTok and many others make it possible for us to connect, buy, sell, follow, engage with and relate to like-minded people, brands, experts and celebrities. Crucially, this technology also gives those of us who want to start a business the ability to test, launch and grow an idea with just a few clicks.

Maybe you already have an idea for a business, or you've caught yourself thinking, 'I could do that' while scrolling through Instagram. Maybe people have told you, 'you're really good at that' or 'you should sell it', or you've seen a product or service that you think could be done better, differently or cheaper.

Not everyone sees these opportunities. Not everyone has a desire to create something from scratch, or a vision to work for themselves. These are sure signs that you've got an entrepreneurial mindset.

So, if you're thinking about it, you should probably do it ... or, at least, give it a good hard crack!

As a business coach, I've had people knock on my door and start with, 'I've had this idea for two years now'. There's nothing worse than endlessly thinking about starting and never doing anything about it!

You will take your side hustle from an idea to a reality. You don't have to be an overnight success, you simply need to start! We'll get you a few paying customers (which is the difference between a hobby and a business) and by the end of this book, you'll find yourself attracting more new clients. We'll then go through the steps needed to take it up a notch and grow your side hustle into a viable business, if that's your end goal.

A lot of businesses fail because people jump straight in, with little or no research about their plan of attack. Even if your business idea is amazing, without testing it out first, you risk losing it all. A side hustle is a safe, easy and effective way to test out if you like running your business, and if there's an audience who wants to buy what you have to sell.

This is an exciting and expansive time to be in business, and a powerful moment in history to strive to do what you love, and to be paid for it. So let's take our passion, creativity and motivation and dive right in.

Chapter Two

HOW TO *Find Your* Passion & Make It A BUSINESS

The best place to start when coming up with your business idea is to look at what you're naturally good at, drawn to and passionate about. Maybe you've started on this and made some money on the side from consulting, selling your art or handmade goods, or solving problems for the people around you using your talents.

A successful business model is when you create a solution to a genuine problem that people are experiencing or come up with an idea that will add value to their lives. When someone is prepared to pay you for this solution or added value, you've got a viable business model.

Research shows that people who build businesses based on a problem they have personally experienced are more likely to produce a solution that will effectively impact other people's lives. We all have skillsets, ideas and solutions that we can offer to those around us. Your job is to get clear on what you are naturally good at and what you have to offer the world, and to build your business around that.

Once you start to get some clarity on what you want to offer, it's important to remember that you're likely to come up against a number of excuses that will hold you back, such as 'I'm not good enough, there are lots of offerings out there, it's too hard', etc.

Remember that you are right on the verge of great change. Running your own side hustle offers you the freedom and autonomy to live creatively and make money doing what you truly love. To turn back now would be detrimental to your success, life, happiness ... and the reason you started reading this book in the first place!

Stay focused on your end goal.

If we tried to think of a *GOOD IDEA*, we wouldn't have been able to think of a **GOOD IDEA.** You just have to find the solution to a **PROBLEM** in your own life ✳

Brian Chesky

ACTIVITY

Take some time to sit down and journal/brainstorm using the
following questions:

* What do you love to do in your spare time?

* What do people tell you you're good at?

* If you could design your dream day, what would it look like?

* What do you wish you could get paid to do?

* What kind of customer do you want to serve in your own business?
How would you add value or solve a problem in their lives?

* What makes you smile?

* What activity could you get totally lost in, work-wise?

* What are three of your biggest strengths?

* What is your greatest passion?

* What legacy do you want to leave behind?

Once you have your answers, go through and circle any common
themes or recurring phrases. Select four to six words.

Is there a business idea that would allow you to
use these skills or do these activities as a living? Try to articulate
it in one sentence.

Once you have your business idea, ask yourself these questions:

* What problem is this going to solve for other people?
* How would it change somebody else's life?

Now, run it against this checklist:

* Have you experienced the problem that this would solve?
* Do you believe in this idea with your whole heart?
* Does this idea harness an authentic passion of yours?
* Can you imagine yourself offering this day in, day out?
* Are you willing to do whatever it takes to make this idea a reality?
* Would working on this idea bring more meaning to your life?

Did you answer 'yes' to at least one of these questions? If so, you might just have yourself a great side-hustle idea.

Now, Take some time to reflect on what it is you want to do and consider the following questions:

* How will it feel when you see this idea come to life?
* How will it feel when you get your first paying customer?
* What would it be like to see people loving your business?
* How would it feel if you saw someone else bring your idea to life instead of you?
* What would you say if a year passed by and you still hadn't done anything about this idea?

Write out your business idea on a piece of paper and put it in a place where you will notice it every day. Maybe it's the name you're planning to call your business or just the concept of what this business will be. Every time you see it, read it aloud and visualise your business thriving.

Chapter Three

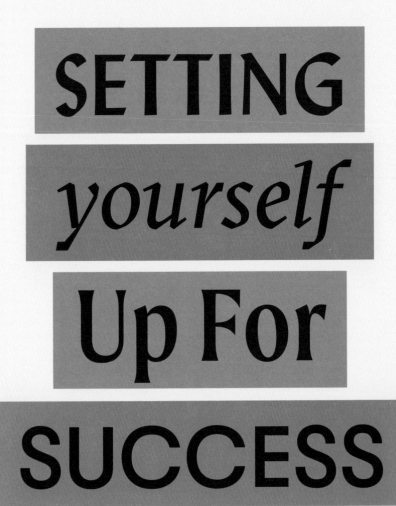

SETTING *yourself* Up For SUCCESS

Building your side hustle will be one of the most challenging and rewarding adventures you'll ever embark on. Like every adventurer, you'll need to load up your with the tools to help you to succeed. Prepare for this adventure by asking yourself some deep, fundamental questions about what you want to achieve.

When you look at any success story, you'll find a team with a well-defined purpose, a commitment to show up every day to do the work, and a determination to never give up on the end goal.

Starting something brand-new and building it from scratch means venturing into the unknown. This can be equal parts scary and thrilling. The good news is that your business success, and your best life, is waiting for you on the other side.

Why?

Why are you embarking on this side hustle? One of the most common traits of a successful side-hustler is their ability to connect deeply to a sense of 'why' they are starting their business. A business with a founder who is not authentically connected to the outcome of why the business exists will likely lack personality and a clear direction. A deep sense of knowing your 'why' will fuel you with passion, determination and a laser focus.

So, what is your 'why' – your reason for starting this side hustle? Is it because you can't believe it doesn't already exist and it will change people's lives? Is it that you want to make a living doing what you love? You don't love your job and you want to design your own career and build your dream instead of someone else's? Or perhaps this business will fund your ability to travel the world? Buy a house? Or work three days a week?

When?

If you're not a routine kind of person, it's time to change!

Nothing fabulous comes without some good old-fashioned hard work, and if you want something different, you have to be prepared to do things differently. You need to get into a good routine that will create space and structure for you to work on the necessary tasks and turn your idea into a living, breathing reality. Let me be honest with you ... this may be the hardest part.

Kickstarting your business will require you to learn new skills, coordinate your efforts and exert a large amount of energy and action to get started. You will build new habits, overcome any fear and self-doubt, and do things you won't always feel like doing.

Who?

No great feat is ever accomplished alone. You will need a team of people around you; people who believe in you and can help make your dream happen. It's important that you surround yourself with people who understand what you are trying to achieve, who believe in you, see your vision and know where you're headed. These people are your cheer squad.

Be intentional about who you share your dream with. This is a vulnerable time, so it's best to limit the number of people who have influence over it. Not everyone knows what they're talking about, some can't be tactful in how they offer advice or opinions, and others might find it hard to listen and support without an opinion. There will be a time for feedback and constructive criticism, but that time is not right now! Focus on positive, trustworthy, clear-headed people who want you to succeed.

ACTIVITY

Your why

Take a quiet moment to sit and imagine the perfect outcome for you and your side hustle. Then answer this question: why do you want to start your business?

Be descriptive and emotive. Write in first person, using present tense 'I' statements that will put you in the goal and allow you to take ownership of what it is that you want to achieve.
I am starting this business because ...

Your when

Look at your planner for the next three months and block out times for when you will work on your side hustle.

Be realistic about the time you can afford, and be disciplined when this appointed side-hustle time comes up. This is your dream, and it deserves whatever uninterrupted hours and energy you can give to it.

Why not?

For most human beings, there's a little voice in our head that makes us doubt ourselves. These undermining thoughts are what many experts call our 'limiting beliefs'. These tend to rear their head at this exact part of the process. When we're on the verge of change, or we're desiring something different for our lives, they tend to become louder, convincing us that you couldn't possibly try something new or create lasting change because, 'you're not smart enough' or 'you can't afford it' or 'you don't have enough time' or 'you're just not the type of person who can achieve that kind of thing'.

The first step to overcoming limiting beliefs is to be aware of them. Once you can clearly see the destructive story you're telling yourself, you can begin to rewrite that story.

How?

Sometimes the most important thing is to just push yourself to do it. This is the difference between people who ultimately make their ideas a reality, and those who don't. You won't always feel like it; your energy levels will fluctuate, and your confidence or enthusiasm might waiver.

What's one thing you can do today to help you get started? It could be telling someone that you are starting or registering your business name or working on your designs or music. It doesn't have to be big or essential; the important thing is to start.

ACTIVITY

Your who

Who are the people you want to help support you on this journey? What are the qualities that make them a good candidate for a spot on your cheer squad? What skills do they bring to your team?

Your why nots

Write a list of all the excuses the voice inside you comes up with. e.g. I'm not smart enough.

For each negative belief, list a counter-thought (an affirmation) that will realign you with your goals. e.g. I am capable and determined, and I can learn the things I need to know.

Your to-dos

Brain-dump everything you can think of right now that needs to be done to get your side hustle started. You want to get it out of your head and onto paper. Don't think about the order or if you're missing anything. I suggest you keep adding to this list as you're working through the chapters. Make time each day to do one thing on your list that will help you to bring your idea to life.

Start before you're READY. Don't prepare, *begin* ✳

Mel Robbins

Chapter Four

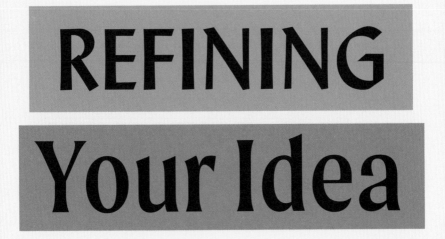

REFINING

Your Idea

Now you have a business idea, you need to dive a little deeper to really understand what 'pain points' it is going to alleviate for your target market and figure out how best to offer it to them.

You already have a top-level idea but in order to make it stick, you will need to dig a little deeper into the needs and wants of those who might be interested in buying what you have to offer. It may sound strange, but your business isn't really about you. Your business needs to be about your customer and what's in it for them. If you hold this clear intention from the beginning, you are more likely to make a real impact on your customers' lives. Subsequently, your business will not only survive but thrive as word spreads that you have a genuine and authentic solution for a problem that people are facing, or that you offer incredible value that people simply cannot pass up. A clear understanding for your customer of why you exist will also help you to make clear business decisions along the way.

Elevator pitch

This is where you start to back yourself! When I meet people who have a side hustle or a business, I ask them one question about their venture: what do you do? At that moment, they have 30 seconds – the approximate time for an elevator ride – to clearly articulate what they're doing and capture my attention with their idea or solution. If you can't succinctly and articulately explain what you do, chances are you're going to miss out on opportunities. If your idea isn't clear in that brief moment,

ACTIVITY

Let's spend some time getting clear on a problem that you have noticed in your own life (if you're basing your side hustle off your own experience) or in the world around you.

* Make a list of problems or pain points that you've observed. Perhaps it's a type of cuisine or consulting service that isn't available in your area, an expensive craft, skincare item or dance class that could be offered by you at a more reasonable price point, or a style of clothing you can ethically make that is currently only made in an unethical way.

* Write your list of problems or pain points down. Then, next to each item, write a business idea that could solve or fix this problem.

* Looking at this list, which of these business ideas is the one you want to make your own? Keeping in mind your capabilities, as well as your passion and excitement levels at the thought of the project.

So, what about you? Tell me in one to three sentences:

* What do you do, why do you do it and what distinguishes you from your competitors?

how can the other person offer you support or advice, or become a customer of, or even investor in, your business?

If you can confidently offer up a clear statement of what your side hustle is, the listener can understand what you do, offer you their business or refer other potential clients to you, or give you useful or even crucial advice, connections or resources.

Market research

In order to stand out and make sure you're properly solving a problem, it's important to consider how you'll deliver a solution that is different to ways that are already available, your clear point of difference. Market research will help you refine your focus, articulate your point of difference, and make sure you're adding something that will really stand out in the market. By looking at similar businesses, you can see that people are willing to exchange money for similar goods or services. Your job now is to figure out why, and how you are going to be different and to find a sticking point that will attract customers to choose your offering over the others. There are billions of people on this planet with different values, attitudes, beliefs and world views, all of which inform who they spend their hard-earned cash with and what they expect from their supplier. You can uncover those beliefs systems and align your side hustle with those who share your interests and values. You can then design the perfect offering so they won't be able to resist!

ACTIVITY

Competitor analysis

List three people, brands or businesses who are currently offering what you aim to offer, or something similar. Now consider what it is that each brand or business does well. Use the table below to help you do your research.

	1	2	3	You
Price points				
Who is their target market?				
Where do they ship to? How much do they charge?				
What makes them unique?				
What is missing from their business?				
What social platforms are they on?				
What is their social media reach?				
What are their strengths?				
What are their weaknesses?				
What trends do they start or follow?				

See if you can notice gaps in how they deliver their offering that you can incorporate into your business to define what your point of difference will be. Next, it's time to turn all this into your brief mission statement or elevator pitch, which will clearly articulate what your side hustle does and why you do it.

Chapter Five

Your customer

It's time to get clear on who exactly will be buying your solution. One of the most important steps when starting a new business is developing a laser-like focus on who exactly your target market is. The most successful businesses deeply understand who they're talking to and whose attention they'd like to capture. If you understand your target audience, you will be able to tailor your business offering to what they need. You need to know how your clients spend their time, roughly how much they earn, what problems they experience, what their general world views are and why they trust the brands they regularly use. This vital information will inform what you do next with your business.

You do not need to be everything to everyone. You need to find and focus on the people that need or want what you're offering. You're never going to please everyone. You want to find those who are looking for what you're doing and convert them into loyal, paying customers. When you get this right, not only will they happily exchange money for your solution, they will return time and time again, and go out and tell others about you.

Humans operate from beliefs and values that are informed by our own unique experiences and interests, and we make choices from an egocentric place. We seek, first and foremost, to understand, what's in it for me? When you're able to deeply understand the needs and wants of your potential customer base, you're one step closer to capturing their attention and convincing them to take a look at what you're doing. If you take the time to learn, you'll earn the right to that attention.

When you try to
be EVERYTHING
to *everyone*,
you accomplish
being NOTHING
to *anyone* *

Bonnie Gillespie

For example, if your business aims to target parents of school-aged children, it wouldn't take you long to observe through your own experience, or through the reported experience of someone you know in this category, the typical schedules and behaviours of people in this demographic. Most would experience sleep deprivation when raising young children, are typically unavailable between the hours of 3 pm to 8 pm as they juggle school pick-ups, homework, feeding, bathing and bedtime routines, and they might have a fairly early weeknight bedtime before getting up and doing it all again. Even just using this preliminary information, we know that if, for example, we wanted to advertise to this target market on social media, we wouldn't be posting our ads during the hours we know they are occupied with their children or likely in bed with their devices switched off. We would then know to aim our efforts at times of the day when they are more likely to be seeking out the solution you offer, and would be in a more ideal state to receive your information and advertising material.

By seeking to really understand your audience, you are better able to serve them and keep them as a customer.

If you can alleviate their pain point, solve their problem or add value to their life – be it joy, status, ease, a way to preserve a memory … then you have yourself a target market.

If you can put your customer at the centre and say, 'How can I help you? How can I be of service? How can I make your life easier?', that person will come back time and time again. And you'll have yourself a business.

ACTIVITY

Let's dive in with some questions to ask yourself about your side hustle and your future clientele.

* What is the problem or need you have identified?
* Who do you think needs this solution?
e.g. a mum who doesn't have time to get to the shops
* What beliefs do they hold around this problem? e.g. what's currently on the market is too expensive or not effective
* Where are they currently looking for this solution?
* Who is offering this solution or something similar?
* What is missing from those other solutions?
* Why would they come to you for your solution?
* How will your solution help them?
* How will it make them feel?
* What five things do they value most?
* What platforms do they use online?
* Where are they spending their time when they are not online? e.g. activities, places and businesses they might be engaging with
* What brands do they love and trust?
* What do they not like?
* What is not-negotiable for them in the brands that they choose to invest in? e.g. ethical, refunds available, a real person etc.
* What is their family structure and/or relationship status?
* When do they shop, where and how?
* How will your solution change their life for the better?

# ACTIVITY

Let's go one step further and get to know your target market a little better. This will be vital information to use to go out and find them later.

* What does an average day in their life look like?

They wake up.

The first thing they do is …

For work they …

Throughout the day they engage on these platforms …

They frequently visit, shop and trust these brands/suppliers …

For fun they like to …

They earn roughly this amount …

They enjoy doing these activities to wind down …

Their social life looks like …

They strongly believe in …

They perceive themselves as …

The frequent problem/s or struggle/s they have in their life is/are …

They are looking for a business/entrepreneur to help them with …

When they seek a solution, they look for …

Talk to someone about THEMSELVES, and they'll listen for hours *

Dale Carnegie

Chapter Six

Branding is telling a targeted audience what you stand for and how you're going to help them. Just as body language, eye contact and facial expressions can help us to understand someone's state of mind without language, effective branding can communicate a message without words.

Most people think that successful branding means a pretty logo, some nice fonts and your favourite colours all put together on a website that immediately appeals to your audience. In actual fact, when thoughtfully executed, your branding will communicate important information to your customer about who you are, what you do and your level of excellence, efficiency or professionalism. Your look and feel, what you do and don't sell, who you work with and how much you charge will all be decisions based on your brand.

When you nail your branding, you will go from seeking out your audience to them finding you.

In order for your branding to be effective, you need to take some time to consider what it is that you want to communicate to your customers. Building a brand will be authentic when the values of that brand are based on what you stand for as an individual.

Values

A brand that has strong core values about what it does and doesn't stand for, and can ensure that the decisions made are rooted in these values, is much more likely to gain the trust of like-minded people and retain them as customers.

 # ACTIVITY

Take some time to consider three brands that you know, love, trust and associate with in your own life. Reflect on how each brand makes you feel, then go one step further and see if you can determine how the company is able to evoke that feeling, experience or belief in you.

For example: Nike aims to make you feel like you can do and be anything. They do this by creating inspirational content that shares stories of people who have overcome hardship and achieved greatness. Their video content in particular showcases extraordinary and diverse athletes, and often includes powerful slow-motion images, emotive music and punchy slogans.

Brand	How does it make you feel?	How do they accomplish this?

A brand is a set of **EXPECTATIONS, MEMORIES,** *stories,* **& RELATIONSHIPS** that taken together, account for a consumer's decision to choose one product or service over another ✳

Seth Godin

In a world of endless options, choices and variety, consumers seek to align themselves with brands that they can build an authentic, ongoing relationship with.

Business name

In order to trade under your desired name, you'll have to register it. The protocol of this will differ from place to place, so to get the right information maybe ask someone who's done it before.

Before you dive deep into your branding, you want to be sure that you can legally secure your business name and that it's not already taken, or you're likely to find yourself in a tricky legal battle. Start with your ideal business name, find the right platform to search if it's available. If it is, register it! If not, most of the time you can play around with the wording and perhaps tack a word on the end, change up the spelling or just start again from scratch. Be sure to do this step before getting too carried away with marketing your business. A few other handy hacks to see if your name is already in use:

* **Google it** – check to see if it already exists. Even if it does and you think you can get crafty with changing it up slightly, you don't want to be too similar to someone in the same field. You'd hate for your customer to come looking for you and find your competition instead.

* **Search social media** – take a look at online platforms to see what's out there in your area. Steer clear of a name that's already in use to save yourself the hassle of trying to secure it legally or getting on the bad side of someone who got there first. It isn't worth the energy it will take unless, of course, it's your actual name. If that's the case, it's best to seek legal advice from a qualified professional.

 # ACTIVITY

First, let's consider the following questions with regards to the values you have in your own life:

* What principles influence the decisions in your life?
* What do you stand for?
* What are your most valued traits and behaviours, in yourself and in others?
* What values do you hold that make you individual and unique?
* What are some causes or issues that you align with and are passionate about?
* What aren't you okay with, or what makes you frustrated?
* What charities/social causes/movements/minority groups do you align with?

Next, decide which of your personal values you want to incorporate into your business stance. Some questions about your business:

* What do you want to be the expert on?
* Use five words that describe what you actually do.
* How do you want your audience to feel?
* What is the purpose of your brand?
* How will you change someone's life?
* What defines the culture of your brand?
* Use four words that describe your business and what you stand for.
* What don't you stand for?

* What is non-negotiable in your business?

* What aspects of your brand will your customers talk about with their friends or family?

* How will your customers perceive the brand?

* What values are essential to the way you make decisions in your business?

* What values will deeply resonate with your audience?

* How will you build trust with your customers?

* Why would they return to you?

* What action are you asking them to take?

* How and where will you ask them to do this?

* What incentives will they have to contact you?

* What makes your brand remarkable?

* Why will people talk about your brand?

* What words would customers use in an online search to find you?

* What are five words you regularly use when describing your business?

* What other interests do your customers have?

* How else can you improve your customers' lives?

Based on the above, research and brainstorm what you and your company stand for, hone it down to four to six clear brand values.

ACTIVITY

Consider which of these aspects of your business are most important to you and the brand that you're creating. What will you be known for by your customers, and which values will you embed in your offering to help you stand out in the marketplace?

* Price point
* Gender, relationship status and sexuality
* Race or religion
* Customer service
* Tone of voice
* Colours
* Images
* Stockists
* Returns policy
* Customer expectations
* Packaging
* Ingredients
* Brand collaborations
* Giving to a cause
* Social media posting
* Marketing dos and don'ts e.g. sales, discounts, alignment with other brands
* Communication e.g. phone, email, online
* The face of the brand

* Giveaways
* Special occasions e.g. birthdays, anniversaries, first-time buyers
* Referrals and rewards
* Office space
* Sales and discounts
* Content creation
* Refunds and complaints
* Staff, contractors and colleagues
* Supply chains, production, sourcing
* Materials and/or ingredients
* Locations, environment
* Promotions and gifts
* The story behind the brand
* Attitude, beliefs and concerns for the wider community/environment
* Dealing with setbacks, mistakes, adversity and change
* Trust building
* Stock, turnaround, exclusivity, availability, urgency
* Delivery of product/service
* Trends you lead/stand by/support

Looking at your list of core values, ask yourself:

* What are the ways I can incorporate and exemplify each of these values within my business?

Chapter Seven

BRAND

Execution

This is where the hard work begins! This is often where the knockbacks, setbacks, investments, wins and losses start as well.

Now that you are clear on your company's values, you can begin the process of packaging it up in a way that makes you proud. In other words, this is where you build your brand.

A brand is made up of colours, fonts, logos, imagery, words and style guides, all of which will inform the way you display your products, deliver your services, present your website, use (or not use) images, develop policies, hire staff, execute collaborations, and anything else that involves the way that you communicate with your customers about what you do and how you do it.

So far, you have worked through the following list:

* A clear idea – the problem you're solving or value you're adding.

* A target market – those in need of this product or service.

* A clear point of difference – where you sit in the marketplace.

* Four to six brand values that represent what your business stands for, and how you will deliver on it.

How are you going to stand out to your target market, tell them what you have to offer, and convince them that what you're offering will be of service to them? Your branding is how you communicate who you are and what you stand for.

This process takes some time, but with a combination of clear intention, like-minded collaborators and feedback, your branding will come together. In order for people to find you, you need to be 'out there'. So how do you get out there? You build your brand, a clear message and you put it in the way of your customers.

We're HUMANS, not MACHINES

Seth Godin

If done right, they should stumble across it, hear about it and eventually come actively looking for it.

You're going to take your brand values and bring them to life in EVERYTHING that you do from here on in. This is where the real entrepreneurs and successful business owners are made – in the action! The ability to get up, back yourself and go out to find real people who will see your value. Not only will your brand portray what you do and how you do it, but it also has the power to become a proud marker of status, belonging, and an outward representation of an inward belief of your customer.

It's time to ask yourself the hard question – how do you do this? The good news is that you don't have to do it all alone! There are many talented creatives out there who have the ability to translate what you want to say into a logo, brand, colour palette and mood board who can help you to communicate your message to the masses. To find these like-minded experts, start in your own circle of influence and see who is playing in the same field as you. If you find yourself stuck, ask around for recommendations from people who have built a business that you love. Social media is another good place to find someone who suits the vibe you're going for.

* Do not judge me by my SUCCESSES, judge me by how many times I fell down and got back up again AGAIN

Nelson Mandela

ACTIVITY

Based on your brand values, what do you know about your customer and their personal values, and the gap in the market that they have been dying for you to fill? What would you like to overhear someone saying about your brand/business? Choose four words that describe how your ideal customer will interpret your business. How will you clearly communicate what you stand for to your customer over various platforms and contexts to help them get to know your brand and what you stand for?

Step 1. Put your brand values across the top of the brand values table.

Step 2. Based on the activities in Chapter Five, when you determined where your customer is spending their time, choose seven platforms or places where your customer will engage with you e.g. website, social media, farmers' markets, galleries. List them down the first column.

Step 3. Starting with the first brand value, go down the table. How will you convey this brand value to your audience across these?

	1	2	3	4	5	6
Touchpoints						
1						
2						
3						
4						
5						
6						
7						

Fundamentals of your brand

Now that you have your mind working on how this is going to look in the real world, you can start to flesh out the fundamentals of your brand. The important thing to note here is that you don't need to go overboard. Sometimes getting in the game is the best thing you can do and, as you start to land your first customers, you can reinvest in the brand to help take it further. This doesn't mean cheap out straight away but do what you can with what you have.

When I first started my business, I made my very first logo in a Microsoft Word document. It was a brushstroke-like font from Word. I stacked the words 'StartUp' and 'Creative' on top of each other and then, using the paint option, I drew a freehand circle around it and exported it as a JPEG file. It was black and white and very simple. Most of what was already in the marketplace was what I perceived as 'busy, corporate, masculine and plain', so I knew I wanted a clean, simple and beautiful brand that creatives would relate to and would stand out. Once I had my logo (which wasn't fabulous, let's be honest) and surrounded it with some fun images, inspiring quotes, funky headshots and a light, relatable and to-the-point tone of voice, I had the base of my brand.

Over the years, as I've gotten in a better position to hire people more talented than me at graphic design, I've kept investing in upgrading my look and feel. As the brand look and feel became more cemented, each time we updated the brand (three times to date), we were then able to charge more money, pitch to bigger clients, and be taken more seriously in the world of business. We seemed to experience an effortless growth in our social media following and an increase in people sharing our content and buying our magazine. The best part? They were exactly the people we wanted to be talking to. Eventually, we stopped going to find them and we found that they were coming to us!

A few things to know about branding

* You will display your brand in everything you do in your business, from your social media platforms and your email signature, to your tone of voice, website and packaging. So take time to consider where your customer is finding you and how they are connecting with you.

* We're doing this now to get you in the game, but it may change over the years. That's okay ... change is a sign of growth. Just start where you are, with what you have.

* Your branding should be consistent across all platforms. The aim is to pick your colours, fonts, image vibe and logo, and rock it across everything you do. Your customer needs to recognise you no matter where they find you – at a market stand, on a flyer in a bookshop, on Instagram, your website or a label on a piece of clothing. It can be tempting to try lots of things out and swap and change with the trends but, wherever possible, build something that is timeless, consistent and easy to replicate across your touchpoints.

* Take a holistic approach and go into all the details. When a brand really nails this, we as customers experience a feeling, emotion or sensation that makes us feel connected, appreciative and loyal to a brand. This often comes in the details. How do you package your items for sending out? Do you write a letter? Do you reply to social media messages or comments? What does your shop smell like? What are you wearing, as the founder, when you deliver your service? You might not be able to cover all of these to your ideal standard from the get-go, but it's good to keep coming back to the drawing board and asking yourself how you can do better.

* You don't need to break the bank. Just like my Word logo, if you're starting with a humble budget, that's okay. Branding is more about the feel, so if you've got a little design skill up your sleeve or perhaps you know someone who can help you out, do what you can to start and come back to it as soon as you can. If you think it deeply and don't just slap something together, your brand will hold a resonance of what you want to portray.

Checklist for your branding

* Make a mood board of like-minded brands, fonts, colours, images that inspire you, make you feel something, and are close to portraying what you're out to achieve.

* Flip back through the exercises you've completed and make a list of words that describe how you want your customer to describe and feel about your brand.

* If you have the budget, you might like to work with a graphic designer or design agency to develop a full-blown branding package, including colours, fonts, design layout and image examples.

* Put your graphics across your platforms to ensure it is all consistent.

* Work with a copywriter to develop the tone of your company's voice and copy (tagline, about the brand, etc.) to display across your platforms and clearly articulate what it is you're out to achieve.

Chapter Eight

MONEY
Mindset

What we **REALLY** want
to do is what we are
REALLY meant to do.
When we do what we
are meant to do, money
comes to us, doors open
for us, we feel useful,
and the work we do
feels like play

Julia Cameron

This is one of the most important steps in starting a side hustle, the one thing that's going to make it less a side hobby and more a viable, long-term business – money. Now that you know what it is that you want to offer and how you're going to offer it, you need to determine what you're going to charge for it.

'What should I charge?' is a question that people often get stuck on. The biggest reason for this is that there is more to money than the price we put on our product or service.

Creatives often undervalue themselves. They don't yet know how much they're worth and therefore do not expect a fair exchange for their talents. Without a solid return on their investments, they soon find themselves with little to no money, juggling a handful of 'other jobs' to pay the bills, tired, time-poor, uninspired and unable to make ends meet. Eventually, many forfeit their side hustle in order to make a 'real living'. If you're serious about your idea, it's time to get real with money talk because without it, your business simply won't survive in the world of business.

Because you're worth it

It's important to note that most people come from a world where they've accepted their earning capacity based on what they saw the people around them earn. Further, if you've come from a life of earning a wage or salary, it's likely you've had your income set for you based on the average pay scale of that industry. You never had to think about it much beyond that, and you certainly were not expected or encouraged to question it.

In some cases, this is a relief. We get to turn up, do our job, and end the workday/week/month with a pay cheque that is entirely ours and, in most cases, we get to leave work at work. We are not privy to the back end of the business or taught the financials, or even made aware of what it actually costs to deliver the end product or service. So, when we endeavour to start our own enterprise, it can be easy to neglect some of the hidden expenses that are vital to starting up, developing, producing and maintaining a profitable business. Mix this with the simple fact that we may never have earned more than an average hourly rate, it is no wonder that so many of us do not understand the money side of a business and can undercharge for our time and efforts.

If you are experiencing self-doubt, fear or shame around charging for what you have to offer, that's totally normal. Remember that business is an exchange of value for money, and the more you showcase your value, the more comfortable you will get with handling the money side of things.

Once you start to feel it in your body and believe in yourself, we are one step closer to confidently charging what we need to in order to make this side hustle a profitable, and ultimately sustainable, business.

When you are able to observe the story that you are telling yourself (the neural pathways that are firing and wiring in your brain, and are the bases of your beliefs), you are capable of deciding what you want to focus on, and therefore fire and wire as a new belief system. It's powerful and quite magical, really.

When money is an uncomfortable or unfamiliar topic, it can be hard to ask for it, manage it and spend it, all of which are vital skillsets for running your own side hustle. So, if you can get comfortable with the topic, then when it comes to pricing your offering and asking others to invest in it, you will feel more worthy and confident to charge your set price.

Changing your money min[d]

Now that you can see what your own internal money
looks like, you will need to ensure that even if you feel li
unworthy or incapable of earning money for doing what yo
you can rewire your past beliefs and habits in order to establis
a more abundant mindset.

Change your language

Thoughts influence beliefs, habits and actions. One of the most
instant and powerful ways you can change your mindset on
money is to change the way you think and talk to yourself about
it. Start taking note of the thoughts that you have around money
and catch yourself every time you think or say something that
comes from a limited headspace. When you think, feel and say
something (whether it is the truth or not), your body, actions and
behaviours will follow accordingly. Phrases like 'I can't afford it'
or 'I'm not worth it' will limit your ability to find solutions and
see opportunities for how you can make your side hustle work.

Stop glorifying busy

We've all been sold the lie that if we work long, hard days then
we will be deserving of the end result. Hard work is necessary,
but going without sleep, nutritious food, downtime and fun will
eventually stifle your creativity, passion and energy. If you're of
the belief that the harder you work, the better the win, then you
will always find more work to do. The glorification of 'busyness'
has meant that we have accepted that the only way to win at life

ACTIVITY

Take some time to understand how you think, feel and behave around money by answering the following questions:

* When you think about money, how does it feel in your body?
* What were the messages you were told about money as a child?
* How does it feel to ask for money in your life?
* What is the most money you've ever earned?
* How much money would you like to earn?
* What do you believe about people who have lots of money?
* What do you believe about people who don't manage money well?
* What messages did you hear about 'going to work' and making money as a child?

and business is by working ourselves into the ground. And it's just not true. Work smarter and prioritise your workload with what's important to the business moving forward.

Money is necessary and can make lasting change

A common myth is that money makes people bad, self-centred and 'money-hungry'. Let's get one thing straight: money is not bad. You may have that belief because that is what you were taught, have observed or heard throughout your life. But if you enter this process thinking, 'I'm not in this for the money', you are less likely to make money. If you can embrace the fact that a successful business requires you to exchange goods or services for money, and that exchange is what will help you to fund, grow and give back in your business, then you will be more equipped to make, manage and use money for good in your life.

Practice using money affirmations

A simple daily habit to help you change your relationship to money is to tell yourself that you can and will have abundance in your life. Even if you can't see, feel or touch it right now, tell yourself that it is possible. If you can program yourself to think with positivity about money, you can and will have it in your life.

The more comfortable you are with loving what you do and knowing that people need what you have to offer, the more likely you are to get paid well for it. This is where you take back the power in your life and stop playing small, and start exchanging money for your work.

Chapter Nine

You will need to decide where you want to sit in the marketplace regarding your price point. When deciding your price point, start with: what do you want to earn? Often people will go straight to looking at what other people are charging without taking the time to consider the circumstances that they would like to set up for themselves. Starting your own business allows you the freedom to uncap your income. It's entirely up to you as to how you will earn that money.

While money considerations can be a challenging part of starting a side hustle, there is power in getting to know the numbers! Every time you find yourself wanting to shy away from this part of the start-up process, I challenge you to stay on top of your numbers and spend time understanding them.

Getting clear on your business offering

You may choose to work with large multinational corporations or to work with a handful of clients and make your goods or service offering more exclusive. You'll also need to decide the style in which you will deliver your offering. Will it be an affordable, fast turnaround, highly adaptable and accommodating solution to a problem, or are you going to deliver a boutique service offering or one-off style option?

To help you decide, you should consider how many hours you want to work, how much money you want to make, and how much time and energy you have to put into your offering. Once you determine your model, it will inform your price point and market position.

 # ACTIVITY

Answer the following questions to determine where in the marketplace you will position your business offering:

* What do you want to be earning as a personal income?

* What are your financial goals?
e.g. replace your full-time income? By when?

* How many days and/or hours do you want to be working?

* Do you want to sell a digital product and make passive income?

* Will you want to sell locally, nationally or globally?

* How many lives will you impact with your business?

* What is your dream scenario for exchanging your offering for money?

* If you could earn anything in your business, what would that be and how would it look?

* How much does your dream lifestyle cost?

 **ACTIVITY**

Use the following worksheet to consider three businesses that you know of that are already delivering a product or service similar to yours. Place them on the scale to see where they sit. If possible, I'd use a variety of businesses that are somewhat different in what they have to offer. This will help you to determine what existing expectations consumers have of brands and what will be expected of you in the price range that you decide on. You may even notice further gaps in your industry and opportunities to provide more value in your business.

PRICE

Low	Market Average	High

CUSTOMER

Low	Market Average	High

SOCIAL MEDIA ENGAGEMENT

Low	Market Average	High

ATTRACTIVE POINT OF DIFFERENCE

Low	Market Average	High

Where do I start?

The materials you use, any added value you include and the delivery style will all contribute to how much you charge. You will need to keep in mind the values of your target market to ensure they can afford it and it is what they are looking for. If you've found a problem that customers are looking for a quicker, cheaper solution to, then your point of difference should reflect that. The alternative is to produce something that is of higher price, value and quality, and harder to execute. Either way, based on what it costs you and who you are looking to sell to, you can decide where in the marketplace you want to position your goods or services.

Mindset hack

If this exercise highlights an area that you think is too saturated, or perhaps you've noticed a big hole in the current marketplace, you might want to consider tweaking your offering slightly. If you learn something in this process that helps you to see things differently, then you may want to shift your initial idea.

Marketplaces are always shifting. You will need to constantly observe, watch for opportunities and be prepared to move swiftly if what you are offering is not getting traction or you are met with competition. Keep your customer at the centre. If you find ways to better serve them or give them a product or service that doesn't yet exist (think Uber, providing a better quality riding experience with more customer control), then I would certainly encourage you to make small shifts as you go.

The ability to be agile, play to the market needs and see opportunities that haven't yet been met is a powerful skillset that will lead to success. Stay attuned and open-minded in the process and be sure to keep an eye out for new opportunities that might reveal themselves. Each time you take a step on your business journey, you will gain a new perspective and perhaps see an angle that wasn't available to you a few steps earlier. Keep asking questions, seeking new ways of doing and seeing things, and you never know what brilliant idea might appear before you to help you to stay relevant and in demand.

What's it going to cost you?

Now you must determine what it's going to cost you to produce your end goal. From there, you can start to see where you will naturally be positioned in the marketplace.

MVPs (minimal viable product)

It's easy to get into your dream state and start designing a business that has all the bells and whistles. When starting out, you should aim to get in the game with what the start-up world refers to as an MVP, a minimal viable product. What is the cheapest way to get your product or service to an operational point? There will be certain expenses that you can't skimp on and are vital to delivering your offering but don't get carried away with some of the extras that might not be necessary from day one. You can upgrade, invest and splurge on some of the niceties down the track. First, you need to get in the game with something to offer and minimise the risk of losing too much money in the early stages of your business.

Be diligent with your spending and frequently ask yourself, 'Is this expense necessary?' Some of the most successful businesses I know started with the bare minimum and built their way up.

ACTIVITY

Take some time to think of all the necessary expenses required to a) get your idea off the ground, and b) keep it running.

Start-Up Costs	$	Ongoing Costs	$
Total			

* How much will it cost you to start your business?
* How much will it cost you to deliver one of your products/services?
* How much will it cost to deliver five of your products/services?
* How much will it cost to deliver ten of your products/services?

Now that you have an idea of the minimum amount you need to charge to cover your costs, you can calculate your potential profit margin and determine what added value you will include, and consider suggested industry mark-ups. This is what you choose to add on top of your base expenses, and it will determine exactly where you sit in the marketplace.

To begin, figure out how to produce something that resembles what you want to sell without too much financial risk. This also allows for flexibility to shift and change along the way, and will test that your product/service is what your target market is looking for. A smart business mind will get in the game with the bare minimum, test the waters and observe the feedback along the way. Once you have validation that the people like what you have to offer, you can use the profits from your sales to reinvest in the business.

What's it going to take?

There are two types of expenses you incur when starting a business: your start-up costs and your ongoing expenses.

* **Start-up costs** – things you pay for once to get you set up and in the game e.g. office set-up, branding, materials and products

* **Ongoing or fixed costs** – expenses that are required to deliver your product or service e.g. internet, packaging, website hosting, tech subscriptions, printing, accountant, business coach, staff and materials.

Industry mark-ups

There are certain industries that have suggested standards for mark-ups on certain products. Fashion is a good example of this. Most brands in the fashion industry calculate what it takes to develop their product, then multiply that price by 50-60% mark-up (meaning the cost to produce x2 or more). This formula aims to cover the cost of the entire production of the product, how long it took the designer to find suppliers, test the garments, design the product to fit, wear and last, shipping costs for sourcing fabrics, international trips they had to take to find the inspiration or build relationships with suppliers, photoshoots, packaging, tags, labels, time to fulfil your order, staff wages, the years of study or research a designer may have done, and the list goes on.

If you're looking to start a product-based business, find a mentor or like-minded business owner in your industry who you can approach for advice. You can also do an internet search to help you to understand what your industry average mark-up is. You don't have to do what is suggested, but it's good to get your head around how others are operating and give yourself a ball-park figure to target.

Where do you want to sit in the marketplace?

Take some time to figure out what you'd like to charge and where you want to sit among your competitors. Your brand values can be helpful in this process to ensure that what you've set out to build will be accurately reflected in your price point.

How to add value/mark-up

If you are running a service-based business, you may choose to add an additional margin to your price tag based on what it takes for you to deliver your service. You are not only selling your time (which is more valuable than you think) but your expertise. This could include, but isn't limited to, your industry study, experience, networks, knowledge, communication style, structure, plan, vision, previous client's outcomes, opinion and achievements to date.

ACTIVITY

Circle the qualities that best describe how you want to deliver your product/service. You might also like to add your own.

* Lots of clients vs boutique service, fewer clients

* Affordable vs high-end

* Quick vs in-depth

* Highly accessible vs exclusive

* Available vs high demand

* Lots of clients vs specific and waitlisted

* Sell less vs high volume of sales

* Ethical production vs mass production

* Locally made vs outsourced to the cheapest factory

* How do you want your customers to describe your price point? Brainstorm any other words you might use to describe your end product/service.

This is what is called 'perceived value'. The value that lies in you, and uniquely you. It can be hard to price yourself and your time as a service provider because often what makes you good at what you do isn't tangible or seen. Remember that you are selling you, so take some time to consider what you are worth. So many people would rather be underpaid than have this conversation with themselves. Don't shy away from considering what you're worth!

In the upcoming chapter on marketing, how you can accurately portray your value as a service provider, validate your price point and convince your ideal customer to invest in you will be discussed in further detail.

What's your price?

Time to have a crack at your mark-up price! You'll likely make excuses. You're probably saying something along the lines of 'but I don't know what to charge! I'll do it later'. JUST DO IT! And if you're really stuck, try these steps: pick a number and write it on a piece of paper. Say it out loud and test how it makes you feel (if it makes you a little uncomfortable, that's ok). Ask a few friends what they would pay for your offering. Take time to imagine getting paid that amount. And if all else fails, go back to your expenses table and start there with a little extra tacked on.

Figuring out your profit

The profit in your business is the amount of money you make once all expenses have been paid for. If you add up what it takes to deliver your product or service and deduct that from your sale price, the aim of the game is to have money left over – your profit. It's good to get a baseline of where you're at so you can get real with the numbers. If you don't see a profit, you are likely running at a loss. If so, don't stress – that can certainly be handled. Was it the same as what you said you could do? If not, what was the difference?

Testing your business model

How does this make you feel? Are you inspired to produce and sell that number of your product/service? Does it make you feel wealthy or overwhelmed? Can you see yourself working to those goals or does it feel unachievable?

Your business should complement the way you want to work or you will quickly lose momentum and energy. Consider if you're capable of producing big numbers of your product or would you prefer to put your price up to a more premium point and have to sell less so as to still make the same profit. If you found that you've put your price so high it's unattainable for your target market, you will need to go back to the overheads section to bring your production costs down so as to be more accessible.

You are the only one responsible for what you earn. So, if you feel like you're being underpaid, burnt-out, or like there's too much going on and you've got too many clients and they're not valuing your time and energy, that's a good indication to come back and look at your pricing. Things to consider when you get to this stage: does the demand mean that you need to make your services more elite and harder to get to? Do you need to hold a higher value for yourself in your own words so that your clients are more willing and able to invest?

If you're not earning what you want and you're struggling to pay the bills or you're feeling burnt-out, take some time to look at your pricing and figure out what you can do differently to alleviate that. Know that it is more than just the math and the numbers; it's what you think you're worth.

ACTIVITY

Consider these questions to determine your profit margin:

Profit = sale price minus costs/expenses

- ✳ What was your monthly financial goal?
- ✳ How much profit do you make per sale?
- ✳ How many sales can you realistically fulfil per month?
- ✳ Adding it all up, what is your profit?

You now need to decide if the goal you set for your earning capacity is going to add up to what you've decided you will charge for your product/service – are you making an acceptable profit?

	Month #1	Month #2	Month #3	Month #4	Month #5	Month #6
# sale product one						
# sale product two						
# sale product three						
Total						

Now try this formula:

Monthly income goal divided by profit = # of sales you need to be making per month to hit your target.

Money hacks

* **Get a mentor** – if you find yourself really stuck with this stage of the start-up process, a mentor, coach or fellow entrepreneur in your industry is a good place to start. Don't be afraid to ask for help, input and their feedback as to what you should be charging and if they think you're on track.

* **Hold the energy** – you have to be confident in your price point otherwise how can you expect others to be? Whatever price you put on your product or service, be prepared to know your worth and back yourself otherwise you'll constantly find yourself negotiating, discounting your prices and doing more work without getting paid for it.

* **Budget for future expenses** – save some of your profits for future growth in your business. You might start out with the bare minimum, which it totally fine, but if you'd like to one day upgrade your website, branding or add extra value to your business, you'll need to plan in advance for that expense. If you spend everything you make, you'll never get ahead and will limit your ability to grow and scale when the time comes.

* **Adjust your price point based on feedback** – if you find yourself inundated with work and people loving what you have to offer, you might find it's a good time to bump up your prices a little, knowing that the demand is high. In the same way, if you find yourself losing customers once they hear your price, you could consider lowering the price to help reduce the barriers people may have to buying from you. Chat to your mentor, clients and perhaps an accountant to help you make the best decision here.

You have the agency to design how this business works and how much you sell and ultimately earn.

 # ACTIVITY

Consider these questions to help you validate your worth and expertise as a service-based business:

* What value do you hold, or can you add to your product, to add a margin to your prices?

* What past experience do you have?

* What education, courses, books, resources have you explored and undertaken to help you acquire your skillsets?

* What makes you really good at what you do?

* What outcomes or results have you achieved in your field to date?

* What clients have you had and what were your achieved outcomes?

* What makes your offering different and unique?

* How much would you like to be paid for an hour of your time?

* How long does it take you to deliver one of your services? Be sure to consider all the necessary steps you take to get your service ready for sale. For example, a service-based business should consider the work they need to do before the session time (intake forms, emails, hiring a space etc.).

Chapter Ten

YOUR *First* Paying CUSTOMER

You will now need to test your offering in the real word to affirm there is a customer out there is who is willing and able to pay for what you want to offer. This process will also identify how effective your business is at meeting their needs and to ensure they keep coming back for more.

A lot of people get stuck here. Worrying about what people will think or the fear of the idea failing can stop you from taking the step beyond the conception stage. By getting your first paying customer, you will validate that your side hustle is viable – meaning it can do what you say it's going to do, and people will spend money on it. That's what will make this a business.

If you're noticing that you're procrastinating on this: do it anyway! You may never be ready, but without the vital step of testing your offering in the real world, you will never know its potential. A good strategy I use to overcome this is to sit back and think, 'What if I got to this time next year and still hadn't done anything about it?'

How to go about getting your first paying customer

Your first customer may not pay the full price you intend to charge, but they should be someone who would genuinely want what you have to sell. If you just start offering your product or service to everyone and anyone who will take it, it's likely that you'll receive mixed opinions on what you've built. The real value is getting it into the hands of someone who actually needs what you have to sell. That way, you can get genuine feedback and test if what you have to offer will make a real difference in their life. Remember, this is about the customer and meeting their needs, not sticking to your idea regardless of what they have to say.

Time to get you out there!

Going back to the chapter where you characterised your customer, who can you think of that fits this description? If no one comes to mind, you might want to think a little broader to a wider circle of influence – a friend of a friend, someone who follows you on social media or in a group that you're a member of, or perhaps you've met someone in the past who showed interest in what you do.

Sometimes it can be better to test things out on someone who's not so close to home so that you feel more comfortable giving it your all without them having a preconceived idea of who you are. This also allows enough space for them to give you honest and valuable feedback without it feeling personal to either of you.

Where you might find your target market

Chances are you know someone who can help get you started.

* **Post to an online group or network** – where might your target market be hanging out? Join some groups or put yourself in a networking situation where you can let your target market know that you're looking for someone who might need what you have to offer and ask if they would like to test it out.

* **Post to your own social media** – tell people that you're working on something and looking for someone who might be interested in giving it a crack.

* **Tell some people you know what you're doing** – you're bound to come across someone who knows someone who needs what you have. Not only does this make it easier, as you'll find your first customer through a referral, which is a softer approach, but as you start to tell people what you have to offer, the word will spread. Soon enough, you'll have people working on your behalf to get your idea to more of the people you're looking for.

* **Run an ad** – think about where your target market is hanging out and put something low-key in their periphery to see if you can get any bites. You might like to test a few different ways of phrasing your offering to see which one gets the most attention.

* **Put some flyers out there** – don't underestimate the power of a good old-fashioned flyer or poster. Design something that is a representation of your brand and use words that would capture the attention of someone who is experiencing the problem you're going to solve. Then make a promise that you can help and call them to action e.g. get in touch, text, download this etc.

* **Ask around** – perhaps you have an email database from a previous workplace or a book of contacts for people that you know need what you have to offer. Reach out, tell them you're going into business for yourself and you'd love to chat about what you can do for them.

* **Gift it** – for a product-based business, it is vital to your process to ensure that what you have developed is going to work the way you think it will. By putting it in the hands of people who will use it, test it and be honest with you about the results, you will receive valuable feedback as to its effectiveness. Often when you are close to a project or task that you're working on,

which you've been working on for a while, you tend to narrow your focus and lose sight of a greater perspective. By giving your product a test drive in the hands of someone who would likely buy it, you have the opportunity to learn more about how it works, and if the user is experiencing it how you intend them to. You could have missed something or perhaps the experience on their device is different, or they notice opportunities for improvement or aspects of the product that they loved and perhaps you didn't give much attention to. Be careful not to give it to just anyone – be selective and make sure it's someone who will be honest with you.

Have them pay

Aside from gifting, you could ask your customers, even the very first ones, to invest in some way for the exchange of your product or service. Not only does this give you a physical example of what it feels like to be paid for your side hustle, it also makes sure that the person on the receiving end is invested in what you have to offer. Without a fair exchange for your time and efforts, you still won't know if your offering is capable of becoming a real business. You don't need to charge the full price upfront if that feels overwhelming. There is a lot to learn from your first few customers, but keep in mind that as you enter the marketplace, you want to be servicing those who are willing and able to invest in what you have to offer. If you can't find anyone, then that is information too. Ask people why they wouldn't, or can't, invest and use that feedback to reflect on what you've created and perhaps take some time to consider if it might need tweaking. Here's a good way to position it: 'Normally the price is X but as an introductory offer, I'm happy to make it X'.

ACTIVITY

Sit down right now and make a list of where you might expect to find your ideal customer, what you will offer them, and when and how you are going to reach them. If you don't give it a deadline, you won't do it, so let's jump in.

	Where are they?	What will you offer?	How will you reach them?	When will you do this?
e.g.	Facebook Group	50% off first order	Post into the group	This Sunday 8pm

Customer feedback

The reason you start small with just a few first customers before you dive deep into marketing and attracting your full capacity of customers is to test the marketplace and the readiness of what you've built so far. It can be blinding and dangerous to the launch process if you spend all of your time behind closed doors developing a product or service without input from customers. The end goal is to serve them and without them, you don't have a business. Doing this early on, and not overthinking it, gives you time to make any changes or improvements or fixes on issues that you might have missed. This could save you money, time and your reputation down the track. By starting small and testing it on a few people, you will learn if what you set out to do actually works.

Seek feedback from your customers wherever possible, even though at times it might be hard to hear or it might knock you back a few steps. It's better to hear it now than to be naive about how people will experience your offering.

Pitching yourself

A good strategy for landing your first paying customer is to go to them. When you're new to the business game, the people you're looking for probably don't yet know you exist. Be proactive and take your game-changing offering to them so they can discover you and your product.

Pitching, simply put, is your ability to communicate what you are doing and how it will help/add value to the lives of others. When done right, it enables the listener to understand in just a few seconds what you do, if they need what you have and whether you are the right fit for them.

Whether you're a fan of public speaking, talking to strangers or pitching yourself for opportunities or not, this is one of the most valuable skillsets in business. You never know what's around the corner, who you're going to meet, run into or get a chance to talk to about what you're doing. Opportunities will come your way and when they do, you need to be ready to jump on them. If you're unclear about what it is that you're doing or who you are serving, it's likely that you will miss out on landing customers, getting a game-changing meeting or a chance to prove yourself. By having your pitch down pat, you're putting yourself in the best possible position to grow and scale your business with ease, and get more of your ideal customers through the door. The ability to confidently communicate who you are, what you do and how could potentially land you chance opportunities you never thought possible.

Write a winning pitch

A strong pitch is a must-have for all business owners. Here's how you do it:

* **Keep it simple** – when someone asks you what you do, get to the point. They don't want to hear your backstory, they want a one or two-sentence answer that tells it how it is.

* **Confidence is key** – even when you're in the early stages of your business, confidence speaks volumes. If you find yourself in a nerve-racking position or feeling a little out of your depth, you may tend to lose your words, but if you can get something out with a level of confidence and self-assurance, you'll still be in with a chance to win someone's trust. Most of the time, it's not the business we're interested in as much as the person behind it. People want to invest in you. So, put your shoulders

back, hold your head high, make eye contact and pretend you know what you're talking about!

* **Practice** – even if it means standing in front of a mirror, your three-year-old niece or the uninspired grocery store attendant. When given the chance to practice your pitch, take it. Repetition is key and, eventually, you'll find your pitch rolls off your tongue and out of your mouth without you even having to think about it.

* **What's in it for them?** – at the end of the day, people are always on the lookout for ways to improve their own lives and happiness levels. The best way to get someone's attention and hold it is to find out what they need, believe, think or feel, and pitch straight to that. Listening is a powerful tool in business and holds many, if not all, of the answers you need to position yourself as the number-one choice for your customer. When in conversation with people, be open to listening to what they want to tell you about themselves, ask questions and see if you can find a common denominator between who they say they are and what you have to offer. When the timing is right, you can drop your banging pitch bomb and wow them with a tailored solution, specific and relevant to their personal values and needs.

Chapter Eleven

BUSINESS *Back End* & Building YOUR TEAM

There are a few things you'll need to consider when starting your business to help you run your show with ease. You will need to build a team of experts who can help you with some of the things that aren't your strong suits. Every country and, in some cases, state or region will have different legalities, laws and terminology for how this stuff works. You will have to do some research into how this applies to you based on where you want to operate your business.

Take into consideration your skillsets and what you can realistically do yourself while still keeping your overheads low. You may not need all of the suggested experts, so go through and see what is missing from what you know, and consider outsourcing or bringing someone on who can help you with what you don't know.

The quicker you can move through the parts of the business that feel hard or that you don't understand by outsourcing them to someone who is more passionate and skilled in those areas, the more likely you are to succeed. When you try to do it all yourself, you can quickly become overwhelmed and bogged down by the small details that will stifle your creativity and motivation, which has the potential to stop you in your tracks. To help you stay on track, invest in other people's skillsets, and have them tackle some of the less important tasks that don't necessarily require your personal input. This will free you up to prioritise the parts of the business that are dependent on you, and help keep you focused and moving forward. You are the entrepreneur, the founder, visionary and creative in this process. You can't do it all, and if the captain goes down, so will the ship. Build a team of like-minded experts who can help you out along the way, and keep you sailing onwards towards your goal.

Building your team

There will be times (especially early on) when you need to do the work and only you can get it done. But most of what you're out to achieve is bound to require like-minded people who will challenge you, hold you accountable and cheer you on. Surround yourself with people who are smarter than you, believe in your vision, and are not afraid to challenge you to think differently, go bigger or sometimes just take a break.

If you find yourself surrounded by people who don't have your back, remove yourself from the situation. Starting a business is a huge feat and can feel like one steep, long, never-ending mountain climb. You don't need to waste time convincing other people to be on your side, to believe in you and help you on your way; if they're not on board, keep moving.

Business structure

How will you structure your business? Are you going solo or working with a teammate? Are you happy to get by as a solo entrepreneur/freelancer for as long as you can before upgrading to a fully-fledged company model? You will need to find the legal structure you require to set your business up to be operational. The options are solo, partnership, company, social enterprise, charity.

Recommended professional: A solicitor who can help advise you on your best options.

Taxes

You'll need to get a base-level understanding of what the tax laws are in your country. If you're looking to expand into a global marketplace, you'll have to understand what is required of you for that. Get your head around it as soon as possible so it doesn't creep up on you at tax time.

Recommended professional: Accountant and/or bookkeeper.

Accounts and admin

Get organised with your numbers early! You'll need to keep track of the real-time data of your sales and any other hidden expenses that might pop up along the way. This is what is called cash flow. A business without positive cash flow, or a founder who doesn't understand that there needs to be more money coming in than going out (as often as possible), will likely sink. If this isn't your strong point, I highly recommend finding someone who loves this stuff (trust me, they do exist) and have them help you out from day one. You might like to keep it simple with a spreadsheet that you manually enter data into, or there are plenty of great apps and web platforms that exist to help make this easier.

You want to have a system in place that can track: money in, money out, loans, sales targets and expenses.

This will help you keep on top of what you're actually making in your business, see how you're tracking, know when you can reinvest or hire, or when you need to cut back on expenses – all vital information for ensuring the business stays afloat and has room to grow.

Online presence

In order to hit the ground running, accurately communicate your message and start putting yourself and your brand out where the right people can find it, you may want to employ some help.

*If you want to go QUICKLY, go alone. If you want to go far, go TOGETHER

African Proverb

* **Photographer** – if yours is a service-based business that is based around you as a professional, I highly recommend getting some professional photos to help you look and feel the part. For product-based businesses, the same thing goes, but for your product.

* **Graphic designer** – if you didn't get around to it before, now is a good time to consider if you feel confident executing your logo and branding to reflect the look and feel for your price point. If not, you may want to consider enlisting a graphic designer.

* **Website designer/developer** – your website will be a powerful tool in converting interested parties into paying customers and will likely be the number-one place where people will buy from you or inquire about your service. It's therefore vital that it looks and feels on-brand, functions well and reflects your brand message. There are some incredible platforms that make it really easy to design your site from an existing template and drag and drop the features around without needing too much coding or tech knowledge. You could start there and see how you go. You don't need to break the bank on your website. Keep it simple and fill it with information that will help your target audience to understand what you do and how you do it, and convince them that this is the place to fulfil their need.

  If you're not confident in website building and design, I would highly recommend getting help. You simply can't afford to cheap out on this.

* **Copywriter** – If words aren't your thing, pay someone who loves them and can convey your message well. Having someone help you to say what you want to communicate will be a sure-fire way to get you in the game quick. Everyone has their strong points and if you find yourself getting stuck on this, don't waste time trying to figure it out. Constructing copy has the ability to stump people and hold them back. Don't let this

simple step slow you down. Aim to get better and give the job to someone else. You might like to ask them for help with your business name, website copy, social media tone of voice, packaging copy, terms and conditions, email replies, blogs, press releases, and more.

Business coach/mentor

A coach has the ability to help you see the bigger picture, keep you accountable and give you short-cuts along the way. If you find yourself going around in circles, needing someone to bounce ideas off or to help you stay on track with your goals, a business coach is the way to go. Not only have they gone before you in the world of business, but their job is also to believe in you, challenge you and help you find a way through what can sometimes feel like an impossible task.

Staff, interns and a VA

When it comes to growing your personal team, there are a few cheap and easy ways to begin with. Over time, as you look to hire and scale your team, I would suggest consulting your numbers guru. When you first start out, you're likely going to need to do almost everything in the business.

* **An intern** – there are plenty of people who would love to run their own business one day and perhaps aren't ready or don't yet have what it takes; you're one of the brave few who are taking the risk and leaping in. The perks of this are that there is likely to be someone who admires what you're doing and is inspired by what you're creating. Business owners are natural leaders, whether they know it or not. Perhaps there is a super

fan who has been following your business journey or a high-school student who is looking for work experience, or someone who would be honoured to be mentored by you in exchange for working in your business. Don't underestimate the power of a value exchange of someone's time for your knowledge or experience. Taking on an intern in this capacity is a great way to get help in your business and support someone else on their career path, and to share your knowledge and experience, as a nice way to pay forward the opportunities you've gained along the way and support fellow side-hustlers who are looking to get in the game. Please note: there are legalities and best practices around the hiring of interns, so you might want to pick the brain of someone more established in your industry before hiring someone.

* **VA (virtual assistant)** – you have access to a global network of people looking to do work they love and/or are skilled at. Technology, the internet and even apps now make it easier than ever to find people who have skillsets that you need, and to allocate tasks to people across the globe. A VA is someone who works remotely, who you communicate with via some sort of tech platform. It could be as easy as an email and shared spreadsheet or perhaps a task-sharing app. However you choose to set it up, the perk of using a VA is that the work is typically contract or project-based, meaning you don't have to enter a long-term employment agreement and, as they are working remotely, you don't have to spend time and money setting them up in an office or managing their work performance face-to-face. Remember, time is money, so there are bound to be tasks you don't need to be doing that are likely time-consuming and not in your skillset. If you find yourself overwhelmed and bogged down in the small stuff, it might be time to outsource some tasks, while still keeping your overheads low.

ACTIVITY

Make a list of qualities you want in prospective employees.

For example:

* Skills to complement rather than duplicate your own
* Someone who shares your values
* Someone who adds enough value to offset the extra cost

Also think about the soft skills you'll need, such as interviewing, training and managing people.

ACTIVITY

Make a list of the skillsets required to get your business off the ground. What skills are you competent in, and what tasks will you require others to perform? For example:

* Logo design
* Website content
* Manufacturing
* Website design
* Photography
* Tech support
* Social media management
* SEO
* Accountant

Chapter Twelve

Marketing

It's time to take what you have to a broader marketplace and bring in more of your ideal customers. Marketing can be a buzzword that many assume will solve all their problems. People tend to throw money around, employing all sorts of marketing or advertising agencies that promise the world and make you feel like a superstar. The best place to start with marketing is you! You are the founder of this company, the creative brain who came up with the solution or value that you're going to offer, and by reading this book and doing these exercises, you should by now have a pretty decent understanding of who it is that needs what you're selling. You are therefore the most qualified person to find, and connect with, your target market. There is nothing more powerful than a passionate business owner who knows exactly what they stand for and why they exist to serve their audience.

Effective marketing is built on trust and relationships. It is not about shouting at your customer, telling them what you do, and expecting that they'll come running with cash to throw at you. What will work is a soft, subtle message in their line of sight to suggest to them that they might be interested in what you have to offer. You will then take those who are ready on a journey to giving it a go.

You cannot assume that just because somebody has heard of you, follows you or shows interest in you they are ready to part with their time and hard-earned money to trust or try what you've got. Your job is to understand them, get to know their needs more intimately, build trust and rapport, and show up consistently to assure them that you can and will deliver on your promise to make their lives better.

Human behaviour and marketing

With an ever-increasing number of businesses entering the marketplace, consumers have more options than ever before to choose where they will invest their money. As a result, we as consumers are spending more time searching for brands that closely align with our own personal values, which can involve anything from the way they source the goods that are used to produce the end product, to the beliefs and values of the founder; from the way they speak to you – or don't speak to you – to how the goods are packaged and delivered, or the size of the perceived value they will add to your life. Marketing research shows that consumers are forming up to 70% of their opinions and decisions about brands behind the scenes, meaning that we're searching online and reading up about companies and asking around for reviews and personal experience from trusted sources before we decide who to shop with. Essentially, we are getting better at stalking a brand, watching it from afar and deciding if it is the right fit for us.

So, what does this mean for you as a business owner? You have to show up – because even if it feels like no one is watching and caring, there is a lot more happening than you know, and people are paying attention! To do this, you first need to figure out where your target market is spending their time, and then be there. It is much easier for you to go to them than to convince them to come to you. By showing up in their world, you are proving that you understand them. The way a brand shows up at their audience's venues of choice (either online or in real life) will determine if they will be given the time of day and regarded as like-minded and worthy of attention. How you speak, the images you use, the colours, fonts and actions will go a long way in helping your audience decide if you are worthy of their interest and, eventually, their money.

Marketing terms

* **Touchpoints** – touchpoints are the ways in which your customers find you. They're the places you choose to position your business to capture a customer's attention. Consider your touchpoints to be the first encounter with your customer, where you get to make your first impression. You don't need to be everything, everywhere for everyone, and you can't possibly be. You'll end up burnt-out and running around in circles trying to keep up. You can, however, consider where the most effective places to start your journey with your customer are, and go there. Examples include internet searches, website reviews, social media, print advertisements, podcasts, flyers, in-person experiences, shopping centres, coupon apps or influencer recommendations, just to name a few.

* **Lead generation** – lead generation sounds tricky but simply put it is the process by which you seek to find the potential customers who would be interested in your business offering and eventually proposition them with what you can do for them, think letterbox flyer drops from the local plumber. When people start out, they often assume that if they can get in front of as many people as possible, then surely some of those people will decide to buy. Effective lead generation is your ability to get to interested customers who are in the market for what you have to offer. You'll be offering a better or different solution to a product or service that your customers are already accustomed to spending money on. Your job, therefore, isn't to convince people to make dramatic changes, but to slightly shift their perspective and inspire them to choose you over another supplier. A lead is someone who is willing and able to invest in what you have to offer. Once you find them, the work begins.

* **Sales funnels** – this is the ability to take your customer on a journey of small commitments and investments to convert them into loyal fans of your brand and business offering. This is the soft approach I talked about earlier, our ability to capture attention, provide value and, over time, convince our target market to spend money with us. Sales funnels rely on your ability to cultivate your customer's interest and keep them coming back for more as they subscribe, buy and return. Think of it like dating; if you turn up on the first date and ask someone to marry you, chances are you're going to get a 'no, thanks' and you'll never see them again. But if you can court their interest, build trust and slowly increase their loyalty to you, then you are likely to one day be in the running for a more long-term commitment.

* **Call to action (CTA)** – this is the action you'll ask your customer to take. We'll explore what appropriate actions are at each stage of the courting process and, if you play your cards right, how to ensure that your customer will do what you're expecting of them. I know this all sounds a bit creepy, but this sort of courtship is happening with brands all the time, even if you're not aware of it. Every time you double-tap, click-through, download, watch now, book, buy, forward and reply, you are responding to a call to action from a brand that has crafted the experience for you to do what they want you to do.

Content marketing

By seeking to understand your target market, their values and needs, you will be in a position to more accurately align yourself with the people who need what you have to offer. But with short attention spans and literally millions of pieces of content being created every second, you need to work a little harder to ensure that your message cuts through the noise, sticks in their minds and is memorable enough for them to take action on it.

A powerful way to do this is to create unique and valuable content that first and foremost aims to serve people and help them get results in their life and/or business. Your end product or service may aim to provide them with more time, energy, focus or beauty, but to get them to believe that, you have to start producing content that will show them and allow them to test it.

The content you create will sit at the end of your touchpoints. By starting small, with bite-sized pieces of valuable and digestible content, you'll be able to capture the customer's attention and keep them coming back for more. The more they come back, the more content you can give them and, over time, you begin to move them down your sales funnel. Start with low levels of commitment for free, which will teach them something and/or help them to solve a problem in their life on their own, and eventually lead them to more valuable advice and offerings that require a larger investment on their behalf.

Some people will find you and love you from the get-go and have no hesitation in beelining straight for your shop or checkout. This is when you know that you've nailed your communication and constructed a reputation that has built trust in your audience. As more people engage with your brand, products and services, this tends to take care of itself. Think of all the times you've told a friend, 'oh you should follow this person', or perhaps you've walked into a friend's house and noticed a product or piece of art that they rave about, or you see the physical signs in a person that they've changed and you ask them what they've been doing to create that change. These natural referrals and word-of-mouth recommendations are pure gold for a business and something you should aspire to, but in order to gain that level of interest and momentum, you need to win over some superfans and get them consuming what you have to offer.

The best way to design your content is by taking a look at your customer's journey to finding you.

If you are generous with your customer before they even spend a dollar with you, you will build trust and loyalty. This will communicate that you, as a brand, genuinely care about them. They will return for more of what you have to offer and, more than likely, bring others with them. Your ability to 'wow' your audience and over-deliver on your promises will go a long way in bringing together a tribe of superfans who will be committed to you.

When developing your content marketing strategy, think outside the box as to how you might be able to relate to your audience other than just through your offering. This could be inspired by your brand values. For example, if one of your values is being relatable, make sure your captions have a similar tone to the way your audience would naturally communicate. You could also share images on your social media that are light, fun and rapport-building to show that you are like them outside of just your business offering. This could include things such as making a playlist, sharing books you're reading, posting photos of a holiday or simply recommending the best places to get coffee in your hometown.

Where to publish your content

Your website – do not underestimate the power of your website. This is the homegirl of all marketing strategies. A brand's website holds so much power, and not enough businesses spend time, money or energy on making sure it's fabulous. When developed effectively, your website has the capacity to be the most powerful, efficient and hard-working member of your team. It can provide information, a payment gateway, customer service and trust, without you even needing to be involved, and it works for you and your customer 24/7.

Here are a few key assets and functions you should consider to optimise your website's ability to captivate your visitors and convert them into customers.

* **A captivating homepage** – your homepage is your pick-up line. It's the first chance you get to properly capture the attention of your audience. The aim of the game is to keep them reading and clicking through. You want your homepage to be welcoming, to deliver a clear message of why you exist (refer back to our section on pitching), to outline the problems your audience may have and what your solutions are, and to make a promise to effectively help. Keep it simple, clear and to the point. I personally love a homepage with a tasteful mix of font sizes, beautiful images and a simple overview of what's on offer.

* **A strong 'About'** – your About page has so much potential to win your customer over. Consumers are becoming more interested in looking behind the curtain of a brand to understand if it aligns with them. If relevant, include your backstory and outline your values. Keep it tasteful and to the point. And remember, if you get stuck on this, outsource it!

* **Video** – short and sweet video content can be a beautiful addition to a website. If you feel confident speaking to camera, you might like welcoming your audience to the site and giving a brief overview of your offering. Videos tend to do well on a homepage, but be sure to optimise the size so as to not slow the whole site down. If your site is slow there's a high chance you will lose your visitor, and there's no guarantee they'll return.

* **Testimonials** – testimonials not only prove that you can do what you say you're going to do, but they can help ease a buyer's anxiety or scepticism when deciding to spend money with you for the first time. Online customers' trust in brands is on the decline, which means you need to work harder to convince your audience that you're the real deal. Other people's

 # ACTIVITY

First, let's look at where your customers might be finding you.
Where are they spending their time, finding answers to their problems,
seeking advice and looking for added value in their life?
List seven of these touchpoints.

_____

_____

_____

_____

_____

_____

_____

opinions can help you do that because a testimonial is a record of a real-life experience and should be from an unbiased person that will help lend you legitimacy.

* **Blog** – a blog serves many purposes on a website. It is an opportunity to showcase your expertise and provide valuable information to your audience, as well as feature like-minded people who are a reflection of your target market. Blogs also give you a chance to add keywords to your site that will help improve the likelihood of your website showing up in an online search. I suggest keeping blogs short and actionable. Consider making your titles catchy and practical e.g. 'Three ways to _____' or 'How to _____'. The purpose of your blog is to give extra information to your audience, help them find answers and give them a reason to keep coming back to your site.

* **Frequently Asked Questions (FAQs)** – add an FAQs section to your site to break down any barriers, concerns or hesitations your audience may have in taking the final step: buying. This is a great way to assure them that you understand them and are committed to meeting their needs. You'll often hear these questions directly from your audience, and you can continue to update this section of your site as you come across concerns they might have about your product/service. Make a list of reasons people might not buy, and consider extra information they might require to be confident in their decision.

* **Opt-in or lead magnet** – a freebie on your website for visitors to download. It's a way to say 'Hey! Thanks for visiting, we appreciate your time and here's something we have for you'. It's like walking into an event and receiving a free drink on arrival; you instantly feel welcomed, put at ease and open to hearing more. Your opt-in could be anything from a discount code, a checklist, recipe book or print download, just to name a few. Get creative with it, make sure it's of value and sparks the

sensation of 'wow, I can't believe I got this for free'. An opt-in should always require the visitor to enter their email address in order to receive the freebie. This will help you build your email database, which is a highly effective marketing tool.

* **Clear navigation** – there is nothing worse than a website full of out-of-the-box, vague wording that can confuse the consumer. Take some time to experience your website as a user. Ask a friend or colleague to use your website and provide feedback. You want to ensure it's easy to get around, is respectful to the user and naturally drives their attention to valuable information. Don't waste your user's time with junk or distractions. Get to the point, show them what you have to offer, and invite them to shop with you.

* **Optimised for mobile** – all of the above goes for the mobile version of your website too. The majority of consumers are digesting online content from their mobile devices. If you're going to spend time building your social media presence – which you certainly should – then your call to action and click-through will be from a mobile device. You have just a few seconds to hold their attention and get them over the line to make your sale, so if your website doesn't translate perfectly to mobile, you're likely going to miss your chance. Test it yourself, get someone else to as well and, if need be, find yourself an expert that will tidy it up for you.

* **Easy-to-use payment gateways** – this is where the magic happens: the checkout. Depending on where in the world you are offering your goods/services, you want to make sure that your website is capable of taking appropriate payment. There are plenty of incredible tech platforms that manage this side of things for you, and make it really easy to link up to your website and bank account. Test them out for yourself to make sure they are running smoothly on your site and are accessible to those looking to buy from you.

* **Contact form** – if you're in the business of offering a service, your contact form is the initial equivalent of your checkout. You might want to have a number of ways for people to contact you through the website – either a form they can fill out, a contact number and email address, or even a bot that they can chat with directly. Make it easy and obvious for people to get in touch and, when they do, be sure to get back to them in a timely manner. The longer they have to wait, the more likely they are to go find an alternative.

Social media marketing

Your social media platforms should exist to showcase what you do as a business, and your content needs to be able to tell people what it is without needing to use words. Think of it as a mini portfolio that reflects your branding, tone of voice and what you have to offer. I'm also a big fan of throwing in some fun 'just because' content (as long as it's in keeping to the values of you and your brand). Keep the colours, fonts and tone of voice in-line with everything else you're doing, and every now and again, call your followers to action, which ultimately should mean heading to your website to check out what you have on offer. Don't get too caught up on needing to build a massive following. While this is nice, it also has the potential to distract you from your purpose, which is to serve your audience, not your ego. I've found the healthiest way to approach social media is to keep it light-hearted and social; after all, that's why it was created.

How to tackle social media

* Produce unique content including photoshoots, artwork, live videos or captions that feel personal. Always spellcheck and edit before you post.

* Hashtags can help people find you when they are searching for brands or products to follow.

* Be authentic to you and keep a posting schedule that is manageable based on your skillset or relationship with the platform. If you get caught up trying to keep up with others or comparing yourself, it will drain you of energy that you could be spending elsewhere.

* Be a real person and remember that people are on social media to connect and be social with their friends and family as well as to engage with brands. While it's a powerful platform to capture the attention of your audience, you want to play to the style of communication people are expecting. If you're going to be on there, be social, engage with your audience, ask them to engage with you, reply to comments and DMs, ask questions and try to have some fun. It doesn't need to be so serious and overwhelming and, again, not every post needs to be a hardcore sales pitch.

Remember that it is a free platform which enables the privilege of connecting with our audience across the globe with a whole lot of ease, but it is owned and operated by a third party and it isn't guaranteed to be around forever. Use social media as a tool to showcase what you have to offer and ultimately drive traffic to your website, where you can collect email addresses and build your own database that you will own and won't lose if by chance the social media channels crash, disappear or lose traction. Be sure to not put all your eggs in the one basket.

Leveraging other people's platforms

An effective way to market your product or service is to leverage other people's reputation and their audience's trust. If marketing is about getting in front of more of your target market to generate leads, then you should be regularly finding ways to get yourself in front of a like-minded and invested audience that someone else has already built. The best way to go about this is to think of a win-win situation where you can add value to someone's audience or platform in exchange for exposure. When someone has done the hard work of building their audience and earning their trust, their recommendation of you and your business will likely be taken seriously. Spend some time thinking about who is already speaking to your target market, and pitch something of value to them. Make sure it's something that you think their audience would like, and will ultimately spark their interest in you.

Ideas for leveraging other people's platforms:

* **Blogs** – offer to write a guest blog post or be featured as an interviewee on someone else's website. You might like to exchange and offer them the same exposure to your audience.

* **Magazines** – pitch yourself as a feature or contributing writer to a magazine that your ideal audience would already be interested in and reading.

* **Podcasts** – pitch yourself as an expert or guest on a podcast that your audience would be listening to – offer to share your story, advice or helpful information for listeners, thereby positioning yourself as an expert and/or trusted source.

* **Speaking engagements, live appearances and artistic contributions** – pitch yourself as a speaker for a conference, event, workshop or webinar series. This gives you an opportunity to showcase your knowledge, skillset and

experiences to an audience that someone else is pulling together. If you're an artist, you could suggest a live performance, contributions to promotional materials/artwork/ anthologies or creative workshops.

* **Influencers and brand ambassadors** – if you know of someone who has a highly engaged audience that tends to follow the advice they give, you might like to gift or employ them to test-drive what you have to offer, and have them tell their audience about you. When done right, this can be an effective way to gain the trust and confidence of more of the people you're looking to talk to. If you go down this route, be sure to work with people who would genuinely like and use what you have to offer, to ensure that it's an authentic recommendation and that their followers are the people you want as customers, otherwise you risk it falling on deaf ears and you won't see a return on your investment.

* **Press and PR** – if you have a story to tell, get it in the hands of the media, which will get it in front of more people than you likely can alone. You want to make sure your media pitch is catchy and based on an interesting aspect of you or your business. This can be particularly effective if timed to coincide with your launch or a special event.

Choose carefully. The media can be effective in getting the word out there about you but it can also be an over-saturated marketplace that's more effort than it's worth.

Paid advertising

You can't go from zero to hero overnight just because you run a few ads. Marketing is more effective if you take the slow-and-steady approach, so while paid ads can help to accurately target your audience, you can't expect them to go from liking and following to clicking and buying all in the few seconds after seeing one ad. Use this strategy to raise awareness about your brand, show your audience that you exist, and collect data. Once you have their attention, keep showing up with your valuable content and expert advice and, over time, the barriers to buying will begin to dissolve, and you'll be in a more valuable position to ask them to purchase from you.

Search Engine Optimisation (SEO) and internet listings

A common myth in marketing is that you need to be ranked number one on internet searches. Internet search engines are just one way that your audience will find you. We've already covered a number of other ways people can, and will, come across your brand, so don't be fooled by the need to go all out on SEO. You can learn the basics of adding some optimising tactics to the back end of your website via YouTube these days and, when the budget allows for it, you may want to invest in an expert that can help to take things up a notch. But when you're first starting out, producing regular content on your website, running some paid ads to your site and getting yourself featured on other platforms that will drive traffic back to your site, are effective enough ways to increase your website traffic.

Collaborations

Like leveraging other people's audiences and finding like-minded businesses or people who are talking to your target market, collaborations are a powerful way to team up with other smart business owners to provide value to your respective audiences and increase your exposure. You'll want to keep an eye out for brands who might be offering something different to you, but speaking to your people, and find a way to deliver something that both of your audiences would want. This could look like you offering your expertise in exchange for access to their database, or a collaborative effort to design a value-add to both of your audiences, like a giveaway or website opt-in. Perhaps you design their packaging in exchange for social media exposure. The opportunities are endless.

The trick to a successful collaboration is finding the right person to work with, and designing a mutually beneficial campaign that is a combination of both of your offerings and is a fair and equal exchange of your goods and services. Go in with a clear goal of what you both want to gain or achieve, and be sure to carefully select who you align yourself with.

Email marketing

It's a wise move to actively and consistently grow your email database. It will be one of the most valuable assets to your business, and allows you the opportunity to show up on a regular basis in the inboxes of your ideal customers with offers, news and prompts that remind them that you're there to be of service to them. Set yourself up on an email marketing platform that will plug into your website and help you to collect and store the data. Then you want to design yourself a newsletter template that you can send out on a regular basis to your database. Think of your newsletters like a newspaper or magazine. Pack it with content that is relevant to the needs of your audience, update them on what you've been doing, offer them invitations to buy your latest products or services, and encourage them to visit your website for content or news that they may have missed.

In-person

If your audience isn't online a lot, don't spend all your time there. If you have a beautiful product that shines when it's held, smelt or experienced, find a way to showcase it in real life to your potential buyers. You might like to run a market stand, set up a booth at a festival or conference, showcase at an expo or put on a live show. Don't underestimate the power of putting your product in the hands of people who need to experience it. And, by the same token, when you as a founder can stand in front of your target market and watch them interact with your product or service face-to-face, you have a beautiful opportunity to witness how it works in the hands of those you'd like to buy it. In the same way, if you're a service-based business, how can you showcase your expertise to your audience and give them a sense of how you work and your excellence? You could consider running workshops or webinars, or pitch yourself to speak at events, workshops or conferences.

All roads lead back to your website

You do not have to engage your audience through ALL of the above marketing tactics. These are affordable and accessible options that will get you results in the early stages of your side hustle. You should review the behaviours of your audience and decide which ones would be most effective, based on where they spend the time and what it is that you have to offer. It's also wise to consider where your strengths lie and start there. If you try to do all of this, all the time, you may find yourself overwhelmed and snowed under, which will likely result in a watered-down marketing message that won't get the results you're after, and will definitely drain your energy. Pick the ones you think you'd naturally be good at, or could get help with, and start there. It's better to focus your energy on nailing one or two of these tactics, and then be sure to measure the success of your efforts to see if it did what you wanted it to. What you measure, you can grow, so do a few good things well and scale from there.

Chapter Thirteen

MINDSET
and
Motivation

Setting out on a journey to create something out of nothing is an incredible feat. Practical tips, tricks and hacks can get you into the game, but at the end of the day, you're on your own. Who and what will you be when no one else is around and the work continues, when it gets hard and you have to find what at times feels like an impossible solution to a mountain of problems? The thing that's going to carry you through the ups and downs of business (and there will be many), the knockbacks, bad days and the never-ending to-do lists, is you and your mindset.

Doing something you've never done before can trigger all sorts of anxieties, fears, self-doubt and good old imposter syndrome. It's important to implement a daily ritual or routine to keep your mind strong. The mind is a very talented trickster. It has the ability to work for you or against you, and it almost never shuts off unless you actively instruct it to. When you learn to master that skill, you draw attention, focus and power back to yourself, and harness the energy you were wasting on doubting yourself and channel it into taking massive action.

There will always be unpredictable events, blockages and setbacks in your life and your business. These are inevitable occurrences that we must all face. But with the right mindset, focus and determination, we all hold the potential to be limitless in our endeavours to create the life and business of our dreams.

Overcoming fear and self-doubt

Starting a side hustle is bound to trigger a number of emotions. From putting your creation out there, to asking for help or investing your savings into your business. You've had a vision for something you'd like to create, build and grow. It's something new, and in order to take it from an idea in your head to a tangible reality, you have to be prepared to do something different. So, ask yourself: is the threat that I'm experiencing right now real? When you're feeling scared, lean back, observe yourself and consider the worst-case scenario. You'll probably find it's not as big, real or scary as you may have first perceived it to be.

Self-doubt sprouts up when we convince ourselves that we're not capable of doing what it takes to get the job done. You are the only one responsible for that voice inside your head, and if you can start a daily practice of catching it when it's rambling away, then you can begin to quiet it down. This will require a daily commitment to tune that voice out and not let it run the show.

When self-doubt arises, here are some hacks to help you beat it.

* **Call a friend (mentor/coach/fellow entrepreneur)** – a mentor, a coach or a like-minded entrepreneur who is also on the journey can be a lifesaver when self-doubt rears its head. In most cases, you want this person to be someone with personal experience who can help you to get a more accurate perspective on what's going on, and remind you that you've got this!

* **Do one thing** – even if the task has nothing to do with your business, by finding something that you can easily accomplish at that moment, you can trigger a dopamine hit in our bodies that rewards us for achieving. The dopamine will physically change your inner state and you can leverage that accomplishment to not only feel more capable but motivated to do it again.

* **Celebrate** – when you are scared of failure and filled with self-doubt, it doesn't take long to spiral into inaction. This will ultimately make things worse. A simple practice to help keep this from happening is to find ways to celebrate how far you've come, to work out how to feel grateful for yourself and the work you've done, and to find things in life to be thankful for.

Gratitude practice

Research shows that people who feel and express gratitude have lower levels of the stress hormone cortisol and are more resilient in the face of setbacks and difficult experiences. By conditioning our brains to regularly, actively notice, and be grateful for, the small and large positives in our lives, you can achieve a more balanced and less reactive state of being. This is significant for everyone and is especially crucial for the wellbeing of a busy business owner, dealing with the everyday minutiae and ups and downs of start-up life.

Beating procrastination

Procrastination can destroy you and your business. We all battle with it most days, whether it be difficulty getting out of bed or not sitting down at your desk to do that one thing you've been putting off, or finding yourself cleaning the house to avoid making that phone call that you know you need to.

Hesitation = pain. Know this! There is nothing more detrimental to achieving a goal than thinking about doing something, putting things off to 'one day' or using phrases like 'I need to, but ...' These are signs that you're procrastinating on taking the action that you know you need to take in order to make progress. You know what this feels like in your body and it's never pleasant. Maybe for a brief moment, letting yourself off the hook and coming up with an excuse as to why now isn't the right time, or you can't afford to, will justify why you aren't doing anything about your end goal. But in the long run, you will find yourself feeling frustrated, stuck, annoyed and down on yourself.

Instead of putting things off, reconnect with your 'why' and do something. There are very few things in this world that are actually impossible. Sometimes things won't work out and you'll have to figure out a new way to make it happen, but to convince yourself that it can't be done and avoid doing anything is self-betrayal. Your job is to take action on your goals every day, even when you may not feel like it. This action is the one thing that will set you apart from those who don't make their dreams a reality. Procrastination is an excuse; don't let it keep you from what you truly want.

Imposter syndrome

'Am I really the person for the job? Somebody else is already doing it, I'm not smart enough, I'm not good enough, no one will take me seriously.'

Imposter syndrome is a sign that you're going after a dream or a goal that scares you a little bit. It's normal to doubt yourself and your capabilities on this journey.

Here are some hacks to overcome imposter syndrome.

* **Catch it** – when and where does imposter syndrome show up in your life? What's the voice telling you? Write it out and become aware of the story you tell yourself. Even if you don't know a way through it yet, you can at least start to notice the pattern of how it stops you from taking action. In most cases, it will come up when you're on the verge of change and taking

Dopamine is a chemical produced by our BRAINS thay plays a starring role in MOTIVATING BEHAVIOUR … In an evolutionary context, it rewards us for beneficial behaviours and motivates us to repeat them ✳

Trevor Haynes

a bold leap into the unknown. Learn to take the metaphorical leap by doing one thing that will take you in the direction of your dreams and goals. Don't retreat back to the comfort zone. Launch yourself into the unknown.

* **Make yourself good enough** – take a moment to think about what it would take to be the right person to run this business? Would it be someone with a certain qualification, skillset or knowledge base? A level of reputation that you don't have, or perhaps you do and you haven't noticed it yet? Whatever you think you are lacking, make a list and then consider: what could I do today to upskill and feel more confident in getting myself out there? It could be as simple as employing a coach to help you in the areas of business that you're lacking, or sending your work to a mentor who can give you some honest feedback. Be careful here not to make such a long list of unachievable tasks that you'll be forever distracted from doing the actual work. These actions should co-exist with your working life and not bring them to a halt. As you learn and grow, incorporate the useful new things you know into your business and watch as you begin to see the results of your efforts.

* **Daring greatly** – there's an oft-quoted speech by US President Theodore Roosevelt, where he notes that praise doesn't belong to critics or naysayers, but to the person who knows great enthusiasms, the great devotions; who spends himself in a worthy cause; who at the best knows in the end the triumph of high achievement, and who at the worst, if he fails, at least fails while daring greatly'. So, with enthusiasm and devotion, let's go.

Chapter Fourteen

GOAL
Setting

At this point, you should be feeling pretty confident about what you want to birth into the world of business. The aim now is to keep on track with where you're going, and to set some measurable and inspiring goals. Setting a goal allows you to get laser-focused on the direction you'd like to take, and makes it easier for you to channel your knowledge, resources and energy towards a clear outcome.

Imagine what your life will be like in five years from now. The reason we dream five or more years into the future is that it can help our brain to think in a more unlimited way. When we think of what we need to get done this week, month or year, we begin to think logically about what we can fit into that timeframe based on our perception and experience of time. Which for a lot of us, brings up limiting thoughts that tend to trick us into believing it can't be done. We can easily begin to talk ourselves out of it before we even get started.

By dreaming about the future, we allow ourselves to get excited about the possibilities and we can activate an inner drive and motivation to work towards.

In order to take these dreams off the page and bring them to life, you need to get practical.

* **Decide where you're going.** Your 'day in the life of you' journal exercise should have helped you to articulate this.

* **Map out a logical way forward** – go back through your pages from the previous exercise and pull out some tangible goals and outcomes that you can move towards. Read back through your 'day in the life of you' response and pull out three big things that you said you wanted. For each of these goals/dreams you have for your life, list them across the top of the table.

ACTIVITY

Set yourself up in a quiet place first thing in the morning or before going to bed (when our brains naturally move into more of a relaxed state), grab a pen and paper and consider this:

* What would a day in my dream life look, feel, sound and be like?

  Some aspects of your life you might want to cover: business, finances, family and relationships, your lifestyle, health and wellbeing. Write it out in as much detail as you can, using numbers, people, places and names.

  Be sure to write in the present tense. As you're writing, allow your body to really feel what it would be like to live that life. Our ability to conjure up emotions in our mind and body before a corresponding event has happened gives our body a taste of what is possible. When we can really start to feel the experience in our bodies, we can trick our minds into believing that it will come to fruition.

LIFE is like riding a bicycle, to keep your BALANCE, you must keep MOVING

Albert Einstein

	Goal #1	Goal #2	Goal #3
Actions			

Down the side of the table, make a list of the logical steps it would take to bring this goal to life. You can just start by getting anything on paper and then perhaps go back and re-organise the order into a step by step, measurable task.

* **Measure your progress** – remember that what you measure, you can grow. When setting yourself goals, in order to make them feel achievable, you need to find ways to measure your progress and give yourself a clear way of knowing when you've hit your target. This could look like, setting targets of the number of sales you will make per week/month, followers or email signups, new enquires or commissioned jobs or opportunities. This way, you'll be sure to keep track of how far you've come and what more needs to be done.

* **Take action** – now that you know where you're going and what needs to be done to achieve your goal, make a commitment to yourself to do one thing from that list every day. Nothing comes without hard work, and goals are an indication that you want something for your life that you don't yet have. In order to create something new, you have to be prepared to do something new. Some days you'll feel incredibly inspired and ready to take big leaps towards the end goal, and other days you'll have to be okay with doing one small action. Either way, you're still moving towards it. If you find yourself feeling stuck or stagnant, take another look at your action steps and find one thing that you can do in that very moment to move you forwards. Remember, no procrastinating!

Chapter Fifteen

SCALING and *Beyond*

Measure, track, observe, watch

Measure everything. Your sales, followers, enquiries, requests, spending and whatever else applies to your industry. If you can keep track of your growth – be it fast, slow, forwards or backwards – then you can observe what is and isn't working. Not only will this give you a wealth of knowledge about how your product/service is being received, it will also help you take action on trends that you see emerging, and minimise the possibility of losing money, time and resources on things that may not be necessary to your business.

Do your best to understand what the numbers might be telling you so that you can continue to captain your ship in the direction of success. The moment you take your eyes off what's going on, you run the risk of hitting an iceberg that could have been avoided. Stay alert, even when things are going well. This simple habit will allow you to coast into the sunset with much more ease. Stay ahead of the game by keeping a watchful eye on everything that you're doing along the way.

Remember why you started

If the going gets tough, come back to where you started, your why. Why did you start this in the first place, and what are you out to achieve? You may lose sight of it as things get busy. Your customers, suppliers and bank balance will certainly want to pull your attention in all sorts of directions. If you find yourself here,

Luck is what happens when PREPARATION, meets OPPORTUNITY

Seneca the Younger

take a moment to stop, zoom out and reflect on what's actually happening. Is it in alignment with you, your purpose and why you started this business, or have you lost your way?

You set out with a clear goal and a reason as to why you wanted to get into business with yourself and sell what you have to offer. It's easy to get caught up in it all and say yes to things that perhaps you didn't want to do, or things you've learnt are not right for you. It's okay; you can always take time out to realign yourself with your purpose, come back to your centre, and get going again.

It's important to allow yourself space to reflect and be sure you're still enjoying the journey. You'll find that a few simple questions will show you the answers. If you're still stuck, get some smart people in the room and brainstorm with them.

Take stock

Ask yourself: what's working? What's not working? What needs to change?

Make time to work on the business

Your business is like a relationship. It needs time, energy, attention and a surprise bunch of flowers every now and then. When you first start out, it's likely you'll be juggling a lot of tasks and wearing all the hats. You may feel like there is not enough time in the day, and there will be moments when you feel like the ship is sinking and that if you were to stop now, it would cause utter chaos. Breathe! Nothing is so urgent that you can't take time to stop, reset and recharge.

A good practice to get into every so often is to stop working in the business (doing the things that produce your end product) and work on the business (consider what direction you'll take next). You may reach a point where you're ready to take things up a notch, and you'll need to step out of the day-to-day in order to figure out how to grow and scale your business. Or perhaps you're simply just stuck in a never-ending cycle of 'doing'. Both of these are potentially pivotal moments in the business that, without the proper attention, could be fatal to your success. When you find yourself in this stage, take the afternoon, day, week, month or even year off to get an unemotional bird's-eye view on where you're heading, and what you'll need to help you get there. Also, this could be a great time to leverage some like-minded, creative and smart minds that can perhaps see things that you've missed or have not yet imagined were possible.

Set your goals and targets regularly

Keep coming back to your goals and be prepared to pivot along the way. Yes, it's good to have an idea of where you want to be going, but life is ever changing, and you will be faced with challenges that require you to scrap an idea, come up with a new one and find a new solution.

Keep learning

To stay in the game and build this side hustle of yours into a viable business that can, and will, provide your main source of income, you must commit yourself to growth. What you know now will get you in the game, but in order to stay relevant, be taken seriously and outwit competitors who will come along to challenge you, you must continue to educate yourself and evolve.

✳ The tragedy of life is not found in **FAILURE** but **COMPLACENCY**. Not in you doing too much, but doing too *LITTLE*. Not in your living above your means, but below your **CAPACITY**. It's not **FAILURE** but aiming too low, that is life's greatest tragedy

Benjamin Elijah Mays

Make time to regularly upskill and prepare yourself for the future of your business. There is always more to learn and your acquisition of knowledge, networks and skills will only add value to everything you do. Surround yourself with like-minded people who believe in you and what you're doing.

Take your audience with you

Your business exists to serve your customer. As you grow and scale your side hustle, remember to take them on the journey with you. Stay connected to their needs, feedback, likes and dislikes, and position your business offering to best serve them. As you grow, share the journey with them, say thank you, reward them and show your appreciation for their support. Without them, you do not have a business.

Over time, you'll find yourself reaching your capacity. If you reach capacity or burnout, you may want to revise your offering and consider pivoting from mass market to boutique. Find ways to automate what you can, bring on like-minded people to help you serve more of those who need and want what you have to offer, and keep going out to find more of those who don't yet know about you. It is much easier to regularly show up and 'wow' a customer base that you've already built trust with, and offer them new and exciting experiences, products and services, than it is to convince new people to come over to your side. The more you can show up for those who are already giving you their attention, the more they will choose to spend with you and, eventually, they will likely go out and find more of your ideal customer for you and bring them your way. Keep your customer front and centre and seek to be the best solution for the problems they have. Watch as they become superfans who will want to tell the world about you.

Thank You

While my name is on the front cover of this book, it truly was a collective effort that made this publication possible. A huge thank you to Alice, and the Hardie Grant team, for making this dream a reality and for trusting me to produce this pocket guide for the world.

I could not have done this without my little sister and best friend, Emel. You read every word I wrote, made them better and walked by my side every step of the way. Thank you for helping me to believe in myself and tirelessly editing and offering valuable feedback.

Abigail Ulman, my writing coach, mentor and saviour. On days when I made no sense and couldn't get the words out, your magic touch transformed them into a clear and digestible message; I am so grateful to have had you on this journey. To those who checked in on me, cheered me on, fed me coffee and wine and kept me sane on the early mornings, long days and late nights: Daisy Clementine, Emma Power and The Studd family – thank you for helping me to stay grounded and focused on the writing journey. To my parents, thank you for teaching me to dream big, to consistently push myself outside of my comfort zone, and to use my skills to be of service to others. And lastly to our StartUp Creative community. Thank you for giving me the opportunity to turn what I love into a viable business, for trusting me with your startup and business dreams and journeying with me over the past five years, giving me the knowledge and experience to make this book what it is today.

Acknowledgement

StartUp Creative acknowledges the Australian Aboriginal and Torres Strait Islander peoples of this nation. We acknowledge the traditional custodians of the lands on which our company is located and where these words were written. We pay our respects to ancestors and Elders, past and present. StartUp Creative is committed to honouring Australian Aboriginal and Torres Strait Islander peoples' unique cultural and spiritual relationships to the land, waters and seas and their rich contribution to society.

Further Reading

There is a lot that didn't quite fit into the chapters of this pocket guide, so I have developed a resource bank for you to come and enjoy. You can find it on my website www.startupcreative.com. au/book where there are bonus treasures of videos, downloads, scripts and so much more to help you on your journey!

Be sure to reach out if you'd like more information on business coaching or courses that I offer, and let me know what you do next.

Go get 'em squad! I can't wait to see what you create.

＊ @startupcreative

Published in 2021 by Hardie Grant Books, an imprint of Hardie Grant Publishing

Hardie Grant Books (Melbourne)
Building 1, 658 Church Street
Richmond, Victoria 3121

Hardie Grant Books (London)
5th & 6th Floors
52–54 Southwark Street
London SE1 1UN

hardiegrantbooks.com

 A catalogue record for this
book is available from the
National Library of Australia

How to Start a Side Hustle
ISBN 9781743796726

10 9 8 7 6 5 4 3 2 1

Commissioning Editor: Alice Hardie-Grant
Editor: Libby Turner
Design Manager: Mietta Yans
Designer: Ngaio Parr
Production Manager: Todd Rechner

Colour reproduction by Splitting Image Colour Studio
Printed in China by Leo Paper Products LTD.

 The paper this book is printed on is from certified FSC®
certified forests and other sources. FSC® promotes
environmentally responsible, socially beneficial and
economically viable management of the world's forests.

Hardie Grant acknowledges the Traditional Owners of the country on which we work,
the Wurundjeri people of the Kulin nation and the Gadigal people of the Eora nation,
and recognises their continuing connection to the land, waters and culture.
We pay our respects to their Elders past, present and emerging.

Survive the Modern World

Upskill and expand your knowledge with these accessible pocket guides.

Available now

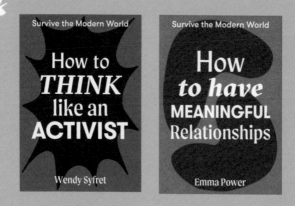